Gross History

Gross FACTS About the Middle Ages

BY MIRA VONNE

CAPSTONE PRESS
a capstone imprint

Blazers Books are published by Capstone Press,
1710 Roe Crest Drive, North Mankato, Minnesota 56003
www.mycapstone.com

Library of Congress Cataloging-in-Publication Data
Names: Vonne, Mira, author.
Title: Gross facts about the Middle Ages / by Mira Vonne.
Description: North Mankato, Minnesota : Capstone Press, 2017. | Series:
  Blazers | Series: Gross history | Includes bibliographical references and
  index.
Identifiers: LCCN 2016032448 (print) | LCCN 2016033568 (ebook) | ISBN
  9781515741534 (library binding : alk. paper) | ISBN 9781515741701 (pbk. :
  alk. paper) | ISBN 9781515741763 (eBook PDF)
Subjects: LCSH: Civilization, Medieval--Juvenile literature.
Classification: LCC CB353 .V66 2017 (print) | LCC CB353 (ebook) | DDC
  909.07--dc23
LC record available at https://lccn.loc.gov/2016032448

Editorial Credits
Mandy Robbins, editor; Philippa Jenkins, designer; Wanda Winch, media researcher;
Steve Walker, production specialist

Photo Credits
Bridgeman Images: © Look and Learn/Private Collection/Michael Godfrey, cover, © Historic England/Private Collection/Judith Dobie, 17, © Look and Learn/Private Collection/English School, 29, © Look and Learn/Private Collection/Harry Green, 27, © Look and Learn/Private Collection/Pat Nicolle, 15, Biblioteca Marciana, Venice, Italy/Italian School, 19, Ken Welsh/Private Collection/André Both, 13, Natural History Museum, London, UK, 9, Photo © Tarker, 23, Private Collection/English School, 21, Victoria & Albert Museum, London, UK/Limbourg Brothers, 7; The Image Works: © Michael Siluk, 11; North Wind Picture Archives, 5; Philippa Jenkins, 24; Science Source/Colorization by Mary Martin, 25; Shutterstock: irin-k, fly design, Milan M, color splotch design, monkeystock, grunge drip design, NatureArtForest, 20, Produck, slime bubbles design, Protasov AN, weevil, Taborsky, 18

Essential content terms are **bold** and are defined on the page where they first appear.

Printed and bound in China
9941S17RRD

TABLE OF CONTENTS

5/17

Dirty Work

In 476 AD the fall of the Roman **Empire** marked the start of the Middle Ages. Life in Europe at this time was difficult and gross. Most land was owned by lords. **Serfs** worked the land from dawn to dusk.

empire—a large territory ruled by a powerful leader

serf—a person who worked without pay on a certain piece of land; serfs could be sold along with the land

Peasants and serfs farmed by hand. This was dirty work. Most people bathed just once a week. Bath water came from nearby streams. These were the same streams people dumped trash and **sewage** into.

peasant—a poor person who owned a small farm or worked on a farm, especially in Europe during the Middle Ages

sewage—human waste that is carried away in sewers and drains in modern times

Gross Fact

Peasants and serfs lived in cramped one-room houses. Farm animals would often share space with family members.

7

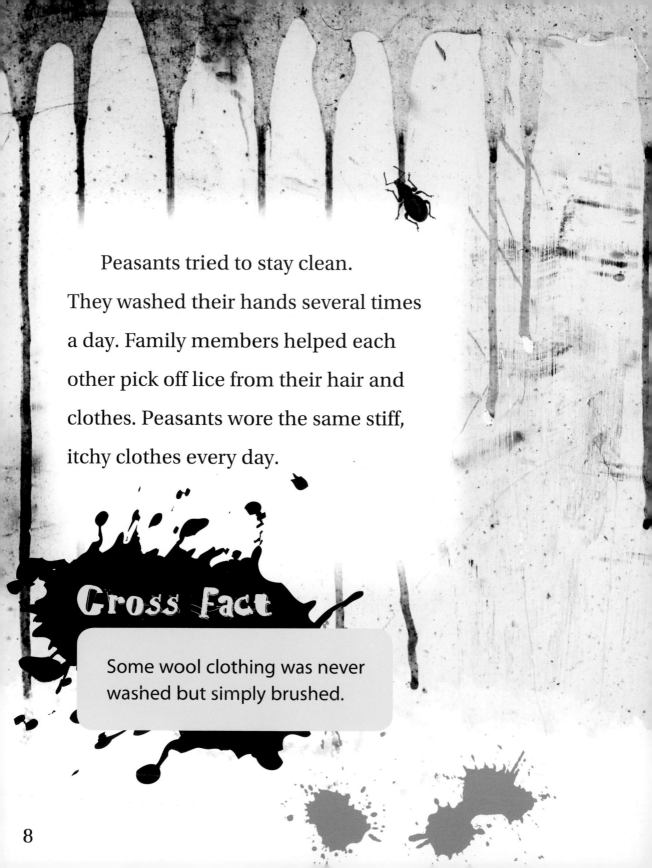

Peasants tried to stay clean. They washed their hands several times a day. Family members helped each other pick off lice from their hair and clothes. Peasants wore the same stiff, itchy clothes every day.

Gross Fact

Some wool clothing was never washed but simply brushed.

9

Rotten Teeth

Many peasants had dirty, rotten teeth and awful breath. People didn't use toothbrushes or toothpaste. Many chewed **herbs** such as mint to cover bad breath. They also rinsed their mouths with vinegar and wine.

herb—a plant with qualities that can treat illness

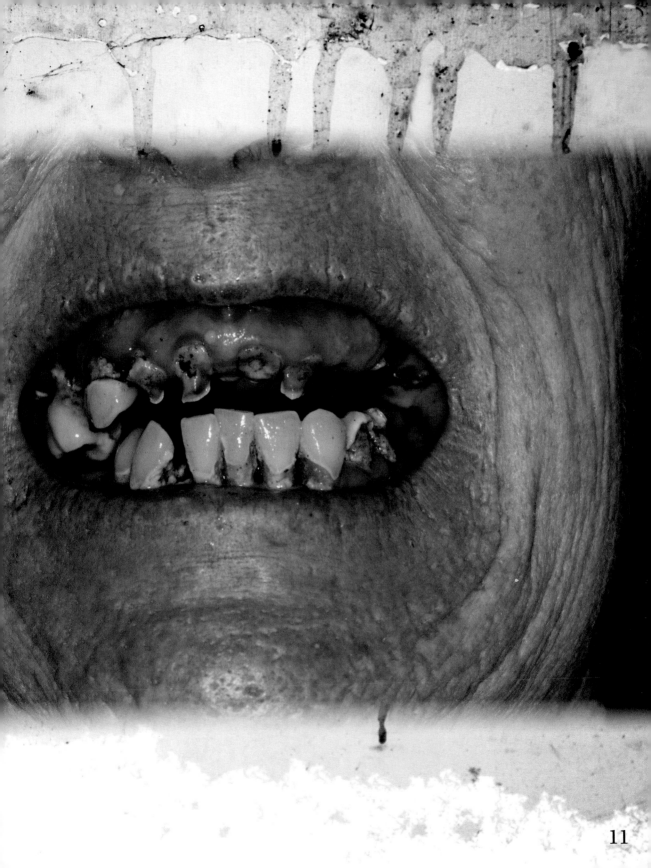

Few treatments existed for rotted teeth. Some people thought worms caused **cavities**. They tried to force out the "worms" by holding an open flame under their jaw. Most people just had their teeth yanked out with a pliers.

cavity—a decayed or broken down part of a tooth

Gross Fact

Rich patients replaced their pulled teeth with fake ones made of cow bone.

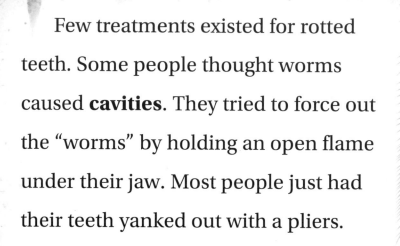

Foul Food

Peasants ate whatever meat they could catch. This included rabbits, beavers, and pigeons. They often dried meat to keep it from rotting. Meat was also stored in a gel made from boiled cow hooves.

Gross Fact

People didn't eat a wide variety of fruits or vegetables. The lack of vitamins left many people with loose teeth and bad gums.

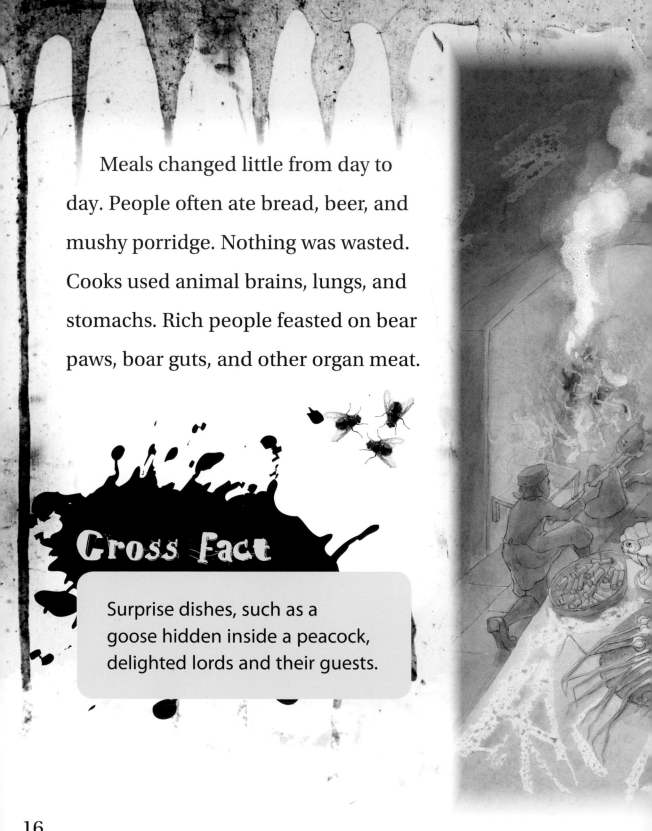

Meals changed little from day to day. People often ate bread, beer, and mushy porridge. Nothing was wasted. Cooks used animal brains, lungs, and stomachs. Rich people feasted on bear paws, boar guts, and other organ meat.

Gross Fact

Surprise dishes, such as a goose hidden inside a peacock, delighted lords and their guests.

Lords sometimes ate meat on **trenchers**. These stale pieces of bread soaked up grease. After eating, the lords gave the trenchers to peasants. For peasants, the grease-soaked, stale pieces of bread were a real treat.

trencher—stale bread sliced to make a plate for other food, usually meat

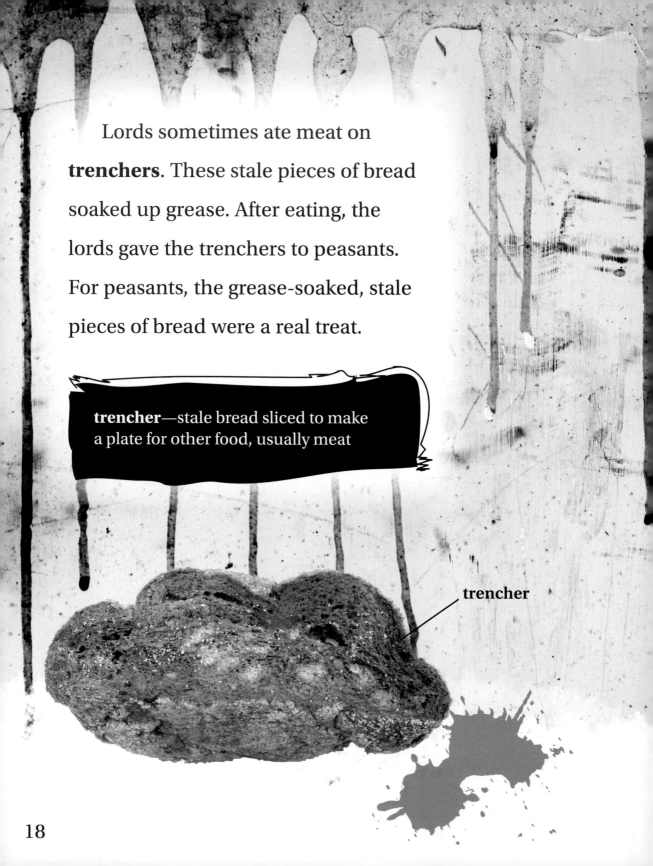

trencher

19

Stinking Cities

Cities in the Middle Ages were crowded and smelly. Trash piled up in the streets along with human and animal waste. Many cities had walls around them to keep attackers out. The walls kept the stink in.

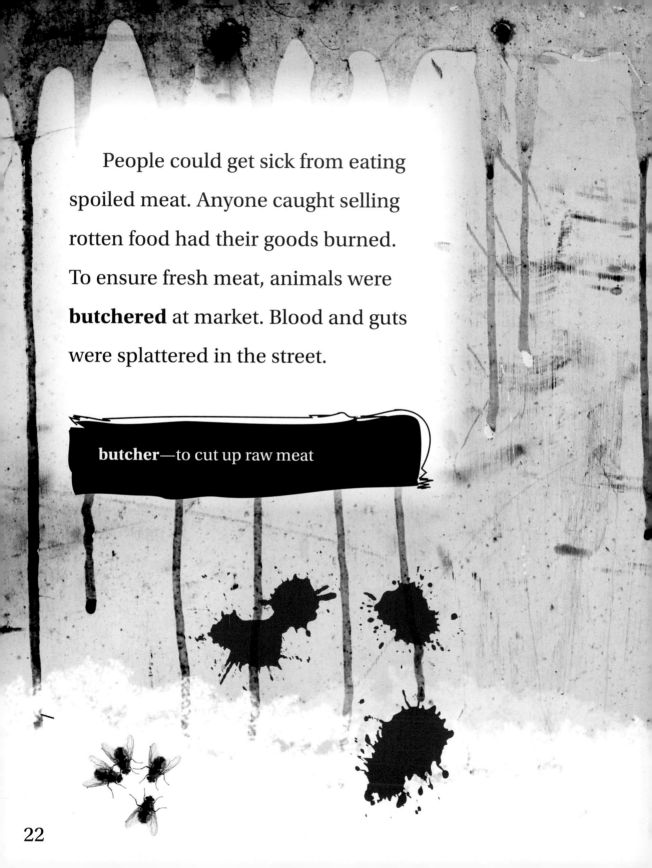

People could get sick from eating spoiled meat. Anyone caught selling rotten food had their goods burned. To ensure fresh meat, animals were **butchered** at market. Blood and guts were splattered in the street.

butcher—to cut up raw meat

23

Don't Get Sick!

People had little medical knowledge in the Middle Ages. Treatments included eating herbs, chanting, or smearing poop on injuries. Sometimes treatments actually killed patients.

herbs

Gross Fact

One treatment for sickness was bloodletting. Doctors sliced open a person's vein to release "bad blood." The treatment could kill people.

The Black Death hit Europe in the mid-1300s. This deadly **plague** killed nearly one-third of all Europeans. The first sign was usually a small, black bump. Once the bump appeared, the plague could kill within a week.

plague—a very serious disease that spreads quickly to many people and often causes death

Gross Fact

People didn't know it, but they caught the plague from fleas.

The plague killed more people than survivors could bury. Bodies were left in the street or dumped in the sea. The plague proved that the Middle Ages were not just disgusting, but deadly.

Glossary

butcher (BU-chur)—to cut up raw meat

cavity (KA-vuh-tee)—a decayed or broken part of a tooth

empire (EM-pire)—a large territory ruled by a powerful leader

herb (ERB)—a plant with qualities that can sometimes treat illness

peasant (PEZ-uhnt)—a poor person who owned a small farm or worked on a farm, especially in Europe during the Middle Ages

plague (PLAYG)—a very serious disease that spreads quickly to many people and often causes death

porrige (POR-ij)—a creamy, hot cereal

serf (SURF)—a person who worked without pay on a certain piece of land; serfs could be sold along with the land

sewage (SOO-uhj)—human waste that is carried away in sewers and drains in modern times

trencher (TREN-chur)—stale bread sliced to make a plate for other food, usually meat

Read More

Gitlin, Marty. *The Totally Gross History of Medieval Europe*. Totally Gross History. New York: Rosen, 2016.

Levy, Janey. *20 Fun Facts About Women of the Middle Ages*. Fun Fact File: Women in History. New York: Gareth Stevens, 2015.

Machajewski, Sarah. *A Kid's Life During the Middle Ages*. How Kids Lived. New York: Powerkids Press, 2015.

Internet Sites

FactHound offers a safe, fun way to find Internet sites related to this book. All of the sites on FactHound have been researched by our staff.

Here's all you do:

Visit *www.facthound.com*

Type in this code: 9781515741534

Super-cool stuff!

Check out projects, games and lots more at
www.capstonekids.com

Critical Thinking Using the Common Core

- How did people in the Middle Ages end up drinking contaminated water? (Key Ideas and Details)

- Peoples' diets were very different in the Middle Ages. Compare and contrast what people ate back then to what they eat today. (Integration of Knowledge and Ideas)

Index